THIS BOOK BELONGS TO

Favorite Picture Books
Illustrated by Gyo Fujikawa

Babies
Baby Animals
Oh, What a Busy Day!
Fairy Tales and Fables
A Child's Book of Poems
The Night Before Christmas
Gyo Fujikawa's A to Z Picture Book
Gyo Fujikawa's Original Mother Goose
Gyo Fujikawa's Original
A Child's Garden of Verses

Gyo Fujikawa's COME FOLLOW ME...

to the Secret World of Elves and Fairies and Gnomes and Trolls

Publishers · GROSSET & DUNLAP · New York
A member of The Putnam Publishing Group
1989 Edition

Acknowledgments

Grateful acknowledgment is made for permission to reprint the following material:

"A Fairy Went A-Marketing" by Rose Fyleman
from FAIRIES AND CHIMNEYS by Rose Fyleman. Copyright 1918, 1920
by Doubleday & Company, Inc. Reprinted by permission of Doubleday & Company, Inc. and The Society of Authors as the literary representative of
the Estate of Rose Fyleman.

"Could It Have Been a Shadow?" and "How to Tell Goblins From Elves" from
GOOSE GRASS RHYMES by Monica Shannon. Copyright 1930 by Doubleday &
Company, Inc. Reprinted by permission of the publisher.

"Faith, I Wish I Were a Leprechaun" by Margaret Tod Ritter from MIRRORS
by Margaret Tod Ritter. Copyright 1925 by Macmillan Publishing Co.,
Inc., renewed 1953 by Margaret Tod Ritter. Reprinted by permission of
Macmillan Publishing Co., Inc.

"A Goblinade" by Florence Page Jaques reprinted from the October 1927
issue of *Child Life*.

"Halloween Song" by Marjorie Barrows from *Child Life*, copyright 1927, 1955
by Rand McNally & Company. Reprinted by permission of Marjorie Barrows.

"The Little House" by Elizabeth Godley from GREEN OUTSIDE by Elizabeth
Godley. Copyright 1932 by The Viking Press, Inc., © renewed by K. M.
Komierowska. Reprinted by permission of The Viking Press and Chatto &
Windus.

"Someone" by Walter de la Mare reprinted by permission of The Literary
Trustees of Walter de la Mare and The Society of Authors as their
representative.

"Song For a Summer Evening" by Mildred Bowers Armstrong reprinted from the
August 1936 issue of *Child Life*.

Grateful acknowledgment is made to Ellen Lenhart for permission to
print her poem "The Tooth Fairy."

A FAIRY VOYAGE

If I were just a fairy small,
   I'd take a leaf and sail away,
I'd sit astride the stem and guide
   It straight to Fairyland and stay.

Unknown

THE FAIRY QUEEN

Come, follow, follow me,
You fairy elves that be,
Which circle on the green,
Come, follow Mab, your queen,
Hand in hand let's dance around,
For this place is fairy ground.

Upon a mushroom's head
Our tablecloth we spread;
A grain of rye or wheat
Is manchet, which we eat;
Pearly drops of dew we drink
In acorn-cups filled to the brink.

The grasshopper, gnat, and fly,
Serve for our minstrelsy;
Grace said, we dance awhile,
And so the time beguile;
And if the moon doth hide her head,
The glowworm lights us home to bed.

On tops of dewy grass
So nimbly do we pass,
The young and tender stalk
Never bends when we do walk;
Yet in the morning may be seen
Where we the night before have been.

Seventeenth Century

THE ELF AND THE DORMOUSE

Under a toadstool crept a wee Elf,
Out of the rain to shelter himself.

Under a toadstool, sound asleep,
Sat a big Dormouse all in a heap.

Trembled the wee Elf, frightened, and yet
Fearing to fly away lest he get wet.

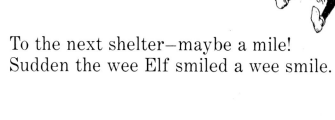

To the next shelter—maybe a mile!
Sudden the wee Elf smiled a wee smile.

Tugged till the toadstool toppled in two.
Holding it over him, gaily he flew.

Soon he was safe home, dry as could be.
Soon woke the Dormouse—"Good gracious me!

"Where is my toadstool?" loud he lamented.
And that's how umbrellas first were invented.

Oliver Herford

Elves

Fairies

Goblins

Leprechaun

Gnomes

Elves

More Fairies

SOME LITTLE PEOPLE WHO
LIVE IN A SECRET WORLD

More Elves

Trolls

A GOBLINADE

A green hobgoblin,
  Small but quick,
Went out walking
  With a black thorn stick.

He was full of mischief,
  Full of glee.
He frightened all
  That he could see.

He saw a little maiden
  In a wood.
He looked as fierce as
  A goblin should.

He crept by the hedgerow,
  He said, "Boo!"
"Boo!" laughed the little girl,
  "How are you?"

"What!" said the goblin,
  "Aren't you afraid?"
"I think you're funny,"
  Said the maid.

"Ha!" said the goblin,
  Sitting down flat.
"You think I'm funny?
  I don't like that."

"I'm very frightening.
  You should flee!"
"You're cunning," she said,
  "As you can be!"

Then she laughed again, and
  Went away.
But the goblin stood there
  All that day.

A beetle came by, and
　　"Well?" it said.
But the goblin only
　　Shook his head.

"For I'm funny,"
　　He said to it.
"I thought I was alarming,
　　I'm not a bit."

"If I'm amusing,"
　　He said to himself,
"I won't be a goblin,
　　I'll be an elf!"

"For a goblin must be goblin
　　All the day,
But an elf need only
　　Dance and play."

So the little green goblin
　　Became an elf.
And he dances all day, and
　　He likes himself.

Florence Page Jaques

THE GOBLIN

A goblin lives in our house,
　　in our house, in our house
A goblin lives in our house
　　all the year round.
He bumps
And he jumps
And he stumps.
He knocks
And he rocks
And he rattles at the locks.
A goblin lives in our house,
　　in our house, in our house,
A goblin lives in our house
　　all the year round.

from the French

THE LONELY ELF-LADY

Down in the bottom of the garden, almost forgotten, stands an old and withered tree. But among its gnarled roots, hidden by weeds, there once lived a little old elf-lady by the name of Mrs. Small.

Mrs. Small lived alone, cheerfully doing her housework, tending her garden, and cooking elfin dishes for her friends, who were many.

But for all her good humor and popularity, she was often wistful and a little bit sad...for Mrs. Small was lonely. She loved her friends, but she was lonely for a family—her very own family. Frog and Squirrel and Bird and Mouse, even Snail all had families that they loved and cherished. But there was no one to share Mrs. Small's pleasant home and agreeable life.

"Oh, dear," she sighed. "If only I had someone to cook and care for...if I had my own family!"

And so the days passed.

One day, as she bustled about the house, she heard a gentle knock on the door.

She called out,

"Who's there?"

"Woof, woof!" she heard.

When Mrs. Small opened the door, there stood a tiny elf-dog, wagging its tiny tail.

"Woof, woof," he said. "My name is George. I understand you are lonely. May I keep you company?"

Mrs. Small was delighted. "Yes, yes, come in, come in!" she said. "I've been longing for company. How nice of you to come!"

So, over a cup of tea and tiny elfin cookies, they talked of this and that and became acquainted.

In no time, George was Mrs. Small's devoted friend. As for Mrs. Small, she greatly enjoyed doing things for George, like making delicious elfin dishes that George might like.

And so the days passed.

One day, they heard a scratching at the door.

George and Mrs. Small listened for a moment. Then she called out,

"Who's there?"

"Meow!" they heard.

When they opened the door, there sat a tiny elf-kitten!

"Meow, meow! My name is Tibby. I heard you were lonely. So I came to keep you company!"

"Oh, how very nice of you. Do come in and have a cup of tea!" said Mrs. Small.

So the three of them talked of this and that over tea and tasty elfin cookies. And, of course, Tibby became a part of the family in no time at all.

And Mrs. Small cooked special elfin dishes that Tibby might like!

It goes without saying that Mrs. Small was most happy for her good fortune. Her days were full of contentment and she couldn't have wished for more.

And so the days passed.

One snowy evening, as they sat talking by the fire, they heard a tiny sound.

"It must be the wind blowing," said George.

"Or the snow," said Tibby.

"It doesn't sound like either one to me," said Mrs. Small.

"Who's there?" she called out. Again all they heard was a tiny sound.

"Well, we better see what it is!" she said, cautiously opening her front door.

There on the snowy stoop was a nutshell! The sound was coming from inside the shell...it was the chortling and gurgling of a tiny, tiny elf-baby! A note on the blanket said, "My name is Donald. Please care for me and you will never be lonely again!"

"Oh, my, a real live elf-baby!" exclaimed Mrs. Small. "How wonderful! I can't believe it!"

"Woof, woof!" George agreed.

"Meow, meow!" So did Tibby.

They carried the elf-baby into the house and admired him. They talked to him of this and that, and he chortled and gurgled and laughed.

In the days and months that followed Donald grew and learned to crawl, then toddle, getting into mischief and making them laugh. George and Tibby happily looked after him. And, of course, Mrs. Small cooked and baked special elfin treats for him.

Never, ever did Mrs. Small dare to hope for such a fine family. First, George came into her life, then sweet Tibby. And now, Donald! Her happiness was complete...forever and forever!

And if, by chance, dear reader, you find yourself in the bottom of the garden, do pause for a moment and take a long look....You might, you just might see tiny Mrs. Small with her family in the tall and tangled weeds around the old and withered tree.

This is an old fairy tale.

THE TROLL AND THE THREE BILLY GOATS GRUFF

Once upon a time, there were three billy goats, all named "Gruff." One day they decided to go to the hillside to eat lots of fresh grass and make themselves fat.

On the way, they had to cross a bridge over a brook. Under the bridge, there lived an ugly old troll with big eyes, big ears, and a great big nose.

The smallest Billy Goat Gruff went over the bridge first.

Trip, trap! Trip, trap! went the bridge.

"WHO'S THAT TRIPPING OVER MY BRIDGE?" growled the troll.

"Oh, it is only I, Little Billy Goat Gruff!" was the answer in a tiny voice.

"WELL, I'M GOING TO CATCH YOU AND EAT YOU UP!" barked the troll.

"Oh, please, sir, not me! I'm too small," said Little Billy Goat Gruff. "Wait for Middle Billy Goat Gruff. He's bigger!"

"WELL, ALL RIGHT, OFF WITH YOU!"

Soon, Middle Billy Goat Gruff came over the bridge. *Trip, trap! Trip, trap!* went the bridge.

"WHO'S THAT TRIPPING OVER MY BRIDGE?" snarled the troll.

"Oh, it is only I, Middle Billy Goat Gruff," said Middle Billy Goat Gruff in his middling voice.

"WELL, I'M GOING TO CATCH YOU AND EAT YOU UP!" roared the troll.

"Oh, no, not me! Wait for Big Billy Goat Gruff. He's very big!"

"WELL, ALL RIGHT. OFF WITH YOU!"

Soon, Big Billy Goat Gruff came over the bridge.
Trip, trap! Trip, trap! Trip, trap! groaned the bridge.
"WHO'S THAT TRAMPING OVER MY BRIDGE?"
yelled the troll.

"It is I, Big Billy Goat Gruff," said Big Billy Goat Gruff
in his big and booming voice.

"AH HA! I'M GOING TO CATCH YOU AND EAT YOU UP!"
bellowed the troll.

"Is that so?" said Big Billy Goat Gruff. "Go ahead! I'm not
afraid of you!" And he leaped at the troll with his big horns and
tossed him into the brook.

Then the three Billy Goats Gruff went on to the hillside, ate up
all the fresh grass, and got so fat, they had to waddle home.

MR. MOON

O Moon, Mr. Moon,
When you comin' down?
Down on the hilltop,
Down in the glen,
Out in the clearin',
To play with little men?
Moon, Mr. Moon,
When you comin' down?
Bliss Carman

SONG FOR A SUMMER EVENING

Fireflies in the twilight—
The fairies might be there—
Each with a little winking star
Showing in her hair.
And the trees are still, and one
Leaf alone is blowing,
Perhaps a pixie flew from it,
Going where he was going.
Mildred Bowers Armstrong

JUPIE THE SPACE ELF

One evening, just before dark,
three elves named Hob, Nob, and Bob,
heard someone sobbing in a nearby tree.

"Oh, who is it?
Why is he crying?
What shall we do?"
The little elves hated to see anyone
in distress, so they called out,
"Hello up there!
Can we help?
Who are you?
We are Hob, Nob, and Bob."

The sobbing grew fainter and then,
between snuffles, a voice said,
    "My name is Jupie.
    I'm pleased to meet you.
    Don't go away! I'll be right down."

And he
    jumped
    to the
    ground
    beside them.

Hob, Nob, and Bob stared at the stranger.

    "I got left behind," snuffled Jupie.
    "That's too bad! Who left you behind?"
asked the three earthlings.
    "My friends, Orrie and Ari! That's who!"
Then Jupie added, "I'm a space elf.
    "I come from some place up there!"
And he pointed to the sky.

The puzzled earthlings looked up into
the big sky. Then they exclaimed,
    "Oh, my,
        you are certainly
            far from home!"
    "You see," Jupie went on, his voice
still quivering a little,
    "we went for a ride in our saucer,
and when we got to your planet,
we decided to land and look around...
    "Well, we were so busy looking that
we lost each other. I was left behind...
and they went off without me!"

"Don't worry, Jupie," said Hob kindly.
"They'll come back for you!"
   "Yes, you just wait and see!" said Nob.
   "And we'll wait with you!" promised Bob.
   "You will?" Jupie smiled at last.
"Oh, thank you! Thank you!"
   Jupie turned on his headlight, so
Orrie and Ari could spot him from
the saucer, and sat down with his new earth
friends to wait.

   After hours and hours, Jupie suddenly
sprang to his feet shouting,
   "There it is! There's the saucer!"
   At first, Hob, Nob, and Bob couldn't
see a thing except stars.

Then they saw a small, bright light
      coming toward them,
          down, down, down!
Closer and closer it came,
      getting larger and brighter,
      hovering and humming, until it
      gently touched the ground.

Then the hood came up,
   a ladder came down, and
Orrie and Ari scampered out!
   What rejoicing as the
space elves were reunited!
   "We looked everywhere
for you, Jupie," said Orrie,
"flying here, flying there, and
scanning the land below
...but no luck!"
   "We almost gave up," said Ari.
"And then we saw your light!"

   "And here I am. You found me!"
Jupie cried, hugging his friends.
   "Now meet my new earth friends.
This is Hob, and this is Nob,
and this is Bob.
   "I must find a way to thank them.
They were kind enough to stay
with me while I waited for you!"

   As they were shaking hands,
Ari said brightly, "I know!
Let's invite them to go with us
for a visit to our planet!"

Jupie and Orrie cried,
"Wonderful! Terrific!"
   They turned to the earthlings.
"How about it? Will you come?"

   Hob, Nob, and Bob were thrilled.
   They didn't need to be coaxed.
   They piped up together,
   "Thank you!
      We'd love to come!"

So they all climbed into the saucer,
  pulled up the ladder,
  pulled down the hood,
  and with a whoosh,
  they soared away—up, up, up...
toward the stars and who knows what
  new and marvelous adventures!

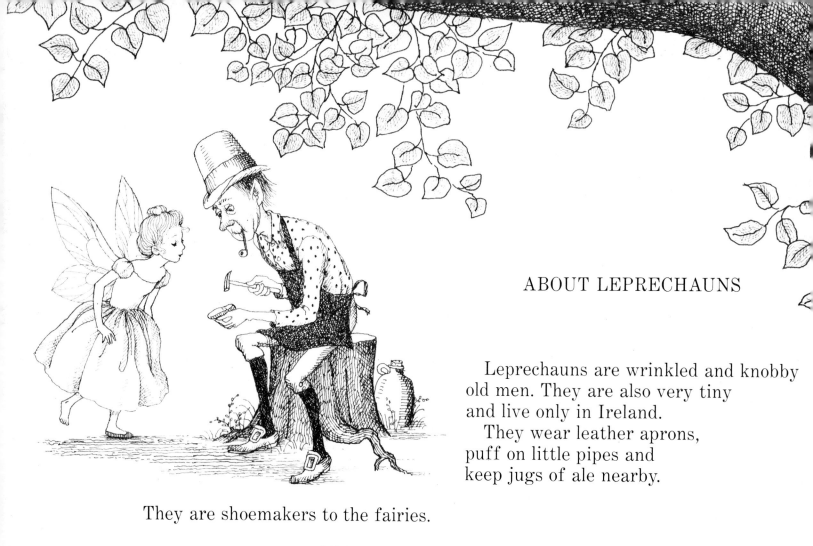

ABOUT LEPRECHAUNS

Leprechauns are wrinkled and knobby old men. They are also very tiny and live only in Ireland.

They wear leather aprons, puff on little pipes and keep jugs of ale nearby.

They are shoemakers to the fairies.

All leprechauns have pots of gold hidden in secret places.

No one has ever been able to trick them out of their pots of gold, for all leprechauns are clever and foxy.

Listen to this story:

One fine day, a farmer in his field almost stepped on a tiny man who let out a tiny yelp, "Ouch!"

The farmer sneered, "Well, well, what have we here? A leprechaun, are ye? Well, then, where is your pot of gold? H'mm?"

"I'm not telling," was the reply.

The farmer grabbed him by the collar and yelled into a tiny ear, "Oh, no? We'll see about that! Tell me where it is or I'll bop you on the head with this shovel! I'm not letting you go and I'm keeping my eye on you, so don't try anything funny. Now, lead on!"

So the leprechaun led the farmer
over hill and dale for miles and miles
until they came to a big old tree.

As the farmer was about to walk under
it, the leprechaun suddenly shouted,

"Watch out! That branch is falling!"

This frightened the farmer and he
let go of the leprechaun.

Of course, it was just a trick.
The branch didn't fall!

But in

that instant,

the leprechaun

vanished

like magic!

And that's how the little old leprechaun
outsmarted the greedy farmer...
and kept his pot of gold!

THE LITTLE HOUSE

In a great big wood
   in a great big tree
There's the nicest little house
   that could possibly be.

There's a tiny little knocker
   on the tiny little door;
And a tiny little carpet
   on the tiny little floor;

There's a tiny little table,
  and a tiny little bed,
And a tiny little pillow
  for a tiny weeny head;

A tiny little blanket,
  and a tiny little sheet,
And a tiny water bottle (hot)
  for tiny little feet;

A tiny little eiderdown;
  a tiny little chair;
And a tiny little kettle
  for the owner (when he's there).

In a tiny little larder
  there'a a tiny thermos bottle
For a tiny little greedy man
  who knows the Woods of Pottle.

There's a tiny little peg
  for a tiny little hat,
And a tiny little dog
  and a tiny, tiny cat.

If you've got a little house,
And you keep it spick and span,
Perhaps there'll come to live in it
A tiny little man.
You may not ever see him:
(He is extremely shy):
But if you find a crumpled sheet,
Or pins upon the window seat,
Or see the marks of tiny feet,
You'll know the reason why.

Elizabeth Godley

ELBERT THE LITTLEST ELF

It was Christmas Eve. The elves in Santa's workshop were in a terrible rush to finish the toys they were making.

In a few hours, Santa would be delivering them to children all over the world. It was very hectic!

While Santa polished his boots, Mrs. Santa ironed his suit. Outside, the reindeer were hitched to the sleigh, prancing and dancing, eager to go!

Everyone was busy. All except Elbert, the littlest elf. He was feeling very left out of the exciting preparations for Santa's journey. He wanted to help, but all he heard was:

"You wanna get hurt, Elbert?"

"It's nice you want to help,
Elbert, but you're too little!"

"Oh, Elbert, I'm sorry you got kicked——"

"Now, Elbert, please go away!"

"You'll only get in the way!"

"Listen, Elbert, get lost!"

"Do you want to get stepped on?"

"Scram, Elbert!"

"Stay out of the way, Elbert!"

"Go sit in a chair, Elbert!"

"Go away, little elf!"

"You're too small!"

So Elbert went
and sat in a corner
and pouted.

"Elbert—out of my way!"

Gosh, all he wanted was to help!

At last, the big bag was stuffed
with toys and stowed in the sleigh.
   From his seat, Santa said,
"Thank you very much, my friends!
As usual, you've done a splendid job!
There's just one more thing. I have
decided to take a helper with me
on this trip!"
   As the elves pushed forward eagerly,
hoping to be picked, Santa saw the
littlest elf, and said,
   "Ah, Elbert, you're the right size!

You're small enough to crawl into
the bag and dig out the toys I'll want at
each stop! So come along, Elbert!"
   Elbert was beside himself with joy!
Now he would be able to help Santa and
have a glorious ride, too!
   All the other elves wished they had
been chosen, but like good sports
they waved goodbye and cheered,

   "Happy journey, Santa!"

   Happy journey, Elbert!"

A NEW HOUSE FOR HILDY

Hildy Gnome was tired of her tiny and crowded house. She wanted very much to move into a new one.

"I need a change," she said.

So she got on her bicycle and went house-hunting.

She drove slowly around the forest, looking at houses.

Suddenly, she braked to a stop!

"There it is!" she cried. "That's the house I want!"

She walked up to a charming cottage in a big tree, saying, "I wonder if it's for sale. Well, there's no harm in asking!"

And she rang the doorbell.

An old gnome opened the door and bellowed, "Well, what do you want?"

Miss Hildy told him she liked his house very much and wanted to buy it.

"It's not for sale!" said the old gnome. "Good-bye!"

"Please," begged Miss Hildy. "Won't you please sell it to me?"

"Nope! Not interested!" And he slammed the door shut. Then he opened it again, saying, "I'll tell you what. If you will wash my clothes, cook, and take care of me for the rest of my life, I'll *give* you this house!"

Miss Hildy was stunned by his offer, but it took her only one second to agree, "Oh, yes, yes!" she exclaimed, "I'll be happy to take care of you!"

So Miss Hildy moved in and became the old gnome's housekeeper. And for awhile, all went well. She washed and mended his clothes, kept the house neat and clean, and cooked his favorite meals.

And Miss Hildy was content.

But the old gnome grew more and more fussy and crotchety. No matter what she did, he found fault and complained from morning to night.

And Miss Hildy became very unhappy.

One day, he threw a plate of stew on the floor! "I'm tired of stew!" he yelled at her.

It was the last straw!

Miss Hildy drew herself up and said firmly, "I have had it! You can clean up that mess yourself! I am going back to my old house and I never want to see you again!"

"Good riddance!" the old gnome called after her as she left on her bicycle. "Now I'll have some peace and quiet!"

"Oh, I do hope no one has moved in," moaned Miss Hildy as she pedaled up to her old door.

But no one was there, except for a stray cat who meowed a welcome as she stepped into her tiny and crowded house, never to leave it again.

For Miss Hildy Gnome was home!

SOMEONE

Someone came knocking
   At my wee, small door;
Someone came knocking,
   I'm sure—sure—sure;
I listened, I opened,
   I looked to left and right,
But nought there was a-stirring
   In the still, dark night;
Only the busy beetle
   Tap-tapping in the wall,
Only from the forest
   The screech-owl's call,
Only the cricket whistling
   While the dewdrops fall,
So I know not who came knocking,
   At all, at all, at all.

Walter de la Mare

THE PRETTY RED RIBBON

"My, what a pretty red ribbon!"
said Teenie, who was Mary's best friend.
"Oh, thank you!" replied Mary,
touching the bow in her hair. "It's my
most favorite ribbon."
And off they went to play in the meadow.

They chased each other around until
they flopped on the grass, breathless and
laughing. And then Mary reached up to
touch her ribbon and found that it was gone!
"Oh, Teenie," she cried, "I've lost
my ribbon!"
They looked and looked for it but they
couldn't find it anywhere.
Mary was heartbroken, for she loved
her pretty red ribbon.
"Mary, don't cry," said Teenie. "We'll
find it, even if it takes forever!"

But they didn't find it because
a little brown bird found it first,
and saying, "How pretty! I can use this!"
flew off with the pretty red ribbon.
She wove it into her nest, and it stayed
there all summer long...

It was still there in the fall when
the little brown bird and her family
left the nest and flew away.

One crisp day, a squirrel,
scampering by the empty nest,
saw the pretty red ribbon
and said to himself,
   "H'm, how nice! I think
I'll take it home to Mrs. Squirrel!"

Mrs. Squirrel was delighted.
   "Thank you, my dear husband!"
she said. "It will add a bit of brightness
to the browns of autumn."
   And she draped it over their front door.

Teenie and Mary never stopped looking for the
lost ribbon. Every now and then Mary would moan,
   "How I miss my pretty red ribbon!"
   And Teenie could only wish with all her heart
that she could bring it back to her friend.

The pretty red ribbon stayed over
the squirrels' door into the snowy winter.
Then one day a gust of wind blew it down.
It swirled and twirled and landed on a
surprised Miss Bunny who happened to be
jogging by.

"Oh, my goodness," she cried, "what is this?"
Then she saw what it was, and exclaimed,
    "Oh, how pretty! I'll wear it on my ear!"
And she tied it on and jogged away.

The pretty red ribbon stayed on
Miss Bunny's ear until the jogging
loosened the bow and it fell to
the ground. This time it lay
hidden in the snow throughout
the rest of the long winter.

At last it was spring.
    The snow melted away and there
on the ground, looking very messy,
lay the pretty red ribbon.
    Along came a wandering mouse.
    "Well, well, what have we here?"
he said, picking up the ribbon.
    "A pretty red ribbon! I'll tie it
on my tail!"
    And off he went through the grass,
waving the red ribbon.

A few days later, on a lovely morning,
Teenie was flitting and gliding about
enjoying the spring sunshine...
when suddenly she stopped in midair!
    She saw something!
        Yes, there it was!
            Bedraggled, but yes,
it was the *pretty red ribbon*!

And of all things! Imagine! It was
tied to a mouse's tail!
    Teenie chased the mouse in and out
between the blades of grass until
she caught one end of the ribbon
and pulled it loose!

And she flew to Mary with it.
Mary was overjoyed to have her ribbon back.
She cried happily,
"Oh, Teenie, thank you, thank you,
for finding my pretty red ribbon! You are
really and truly the very best friend
a person could have!"

OLD NOSEY GNOME

Once there was a gnome who was so curious about everything and everybody that he was known as Old Nosey Gnome. He couldn't help it. He just simply had to know.

So Mrs. Gnome had a hard time planning a surprise party for him to celebrate his 200th birthday! She invited all the little people in the hollow and made them promise to keep the party a secret.

"For goodness sake," she said, "don't tell Nosey!"

On the day of the party, everyone around him pretended that it was just an ordinary day, but Old Nosey knew that something was stirring. He could feel it in his bones.

As he took his walk in the hollow, he saw an old friend sitting on a log.

"What are you doing, friend?" he asked.

"Nothing much," was the answer. "Just sitting. Why don't you sit down too?"

"No, thanks," said Nosey.

Next he saw a couple of elves dancing in the grass and he asked,

"Hey, fellows, why are you dancing?"

"No reason," they grinned. "Would you care to join us?"

"No, thanks," said Nosey.

As he moved on, some tiny fairies flew
past his ear. He asked,
   "Where are you going, girls?"
   "Oh, nowhere specially," they giggled.
"Would you care to come along?"
   "No, thanks," said Nosey.

He was disgusted.
   "Nobody tells me anything! I know
they're keeping something from me."
   And he grumbled on, "I might as well
go home. At least Mrs. Gnome will pay
attention to me."
   But as he opened his front door,
Mrs. Gnome rushed out of the house,
calling back,
   "I have to run over to Mrs. Brownie's.
I'll be back in time to cook your supper."
   "Just when will that be?"
   "Oh—soon..." she said.
And she disappeared down the path.
Old Nosey heaved a big sigh.
   "Oh, well, I think I'll take a nap."
And off he went to bed.

He slept soundly. When he woke up,
the stars were out and he heard the
tinkling sound of laughing voices.
   "H'mmm, what's going on around here?"
he said to himself. "Something is up and
I'm going to find out what it is!"
   Cautiously, he opened the door and
as he stepped out into the night, he could
hardly believe what he saw and heard.

   All the little people of the hollow
   were there, singing,

"Happy birthday to you,
Happy birthday to you!
Happy birthday, dear Nosey,
Happy birthday to you!"
For once, Old Nosey was speechless.
And then Mrs. Gnome led him to a beautiful
birthday cake that flickered and glowed
with light from 200 fireflies!
So this was the secret they had kept from him!

FAITH, I WISH I WERE A LEPRECHAUN

Faith, I wish I were a leprechaun
Beneath a hawthorn tree,
A-cobblin' of wee, magic boots,
A-eatin' luscious, lovely fruits;
Oh, fiddle-dum, oh, fiddle-dee,
I wish I were a leprechaun
Beneath a hawthorn tree!

Faith, I wish I were a leprechaun
Beneath a hawthorn tree,
A-throwin' snuff into the eyes
Of young and old and dull and wise;
Oh, fiddle-dum, oh, fiddle-dee
I wish I were a leprechaun
Beneath a hawthorn tree!

Faith, I wish I were a leprechaun
Beneath a hawthorn tree,
With no more irksome thing to do
Than sew a small, bewitchin' shoe;
Oh, fiddle-dum, oh, fiddle-dee,
I wish I were a leprechaun
Beneath a hawthorn tree!

Margaret Ritter

THE TOOTH FAIRY

The Tooth Fairy is coming
to our house tonight
to take
my sister's baby tooth.
(It fell out this morning!)
Sis put it under her pillow,
out of sight.
I'm going to hide behind the door,
and peek,
if I can stay awake!

Mommy says
the Tooth Fairy will leave
a reward for Sis
under the pillow
(twenty-five cents or even more!).

But I think it's kind of funny—
where will the Fairy get the money?
Ellen Lenhart

COULD IT HAVE BEEN A SHADOW?

What ran under the rosebush?
  What ran under the stone?
Could it have been a shadow,
  Running away alone?
Maybe a fairy's shadow,
  Slipping away at dawn
To guard a gleaming pot of gold
  For a busy leprechaun.
Monica Shannon

HALLOWEEN SONG

Three little witches
Pranced in the garden,
Three little witches
Danced from the moon;
One wore a wishing hat,
One held a pussy-cat,
One went a-pitty-pat
And whispered a tune.

Out flew an owl
Who glared at the kitten,
Out flew an owl
Who stared at the rest,
Dancing, with haughty nose
Each on the other's toes,
Down past the pumpkin rows
Under his nest.

Three little witches
Blew on their broomsticks,
Three little witches
Flew to their queen,
Over the windy glen
Into the night...But then
They will be back again
Next Halloween.

Marjorie Barrows

CHI-CHAN, THE VERY FIRST JAPANESE FAIRY

Somewhere in faraway Japan, there is a certain garden, and in the middle of this garden there is a little pavilion made of bamboo.

On the floor of the pavilion there sits, like an honored guest, a beautiful porcelain dish in which a forest of very tiny trees is growing.

In this forest, one lovely day, there suddenly appeared a tiny fairy. Her name was Chi-chan. She wore a pink and red kimono and her wings were as blue as the summer sky.

Chi-chan was enchanted with the forest and exclaimed,

"Oh, what lovely little trees! And just the right size, too! I will make my home right here!"

She made herself comfortable and spent the following days flitting happily around the garden, waiting to be discovered.

One morning, a little girl came into the garden and ran straight to the tiny trees.

"How are you today, my dear little trees?" she asked tenderly.

As she talked, she glimpsed a flash of pink and red, and looking closer, she spied the tiny fairy.

"Who are *you*?" asked the little girl.

"My name is Chi-chan and I am a fairy. I have come to live with you—that is, if you like."

"Oh, how nice! I'd like that very much. My name is Teru."

Then, looking puzzled, she asked, "But, please, what is a fairy?"

"Well, a fairy is a small someone who is a make-believe special friend to children. We fairies exist only for those who believe in us!"

Suddenly, Teru cried joyfully, "Then *I* believe in fairies! Because for a long, long time I've been wishing for my very own make-believe friend—someone just for me to talk with that no one else can see! And here you are, Chi-chan, to be that very friend!"

"Oh, yes, indeed," said Chi-chan. "You do believe in fairies! That's why you were able to discover *me*!"

And so, from that day to this, wherever Teru happens to be, who is always flitting close to her, playing games and singing happy songs? None other than our tiny friend, Chi-chan, the very first Japanese fairy!

BY THE MOON

By the moon we sport and play,
With the night begins our day;
As we dance the dew doth fall;
Trip it, little urchins all!
Two by two, and three by three,
And about go we, and about go we!

John Lyly

HOW TO TELL GOBLINS FROM ELVES

The goblin has a wider mouth
  Than any wondering elf.
The saddest part of this is that
  He brings it on himself.
For hanging in a willow clump
  In baskets made of sheaves,
You may see the baby goblins
  Under coverlets of leaves.

They suck a pink and podgy foot,
  (As human babies do),
And then they suck the other one,
Until they're sucking two.
And so it is that goblins' mouths
  Keep growing very round.
So you can't mistake a goblin,
  When a goblin you have found.

Monica Shannon

A FAIRY WENT A-MARKETING

A fairy went a-marketing—
   She bought a little fish;
She put it in a crystal bowl
   Upon a golden dish.
An hour she sat in wonderment
   And watched its silver gleam,
And then she gently took it up
   And slipped it in a stream.

A fairy went a-marketing—
   She bought a colored bird;
It sang the sweetest, shrillest song
   That she had ever heard.
She sat beside its painted cage
   And listened half the day,
And then she opened wide the door
   And let it fly away.

A fairy went a-marketing—
   She bought a gentle mouse
To take her tiny messages,
   To keep her tiny house.
All day she kept its busy feet
   Pit-patting to and fro,
And then she kissed its silken ears,
   Thanked it and let it go.

Rose Fyleman

THE LITTLE ELFMAN

I met a little Elfman once,
　　Down where the lilies blow.
I asked him why he was so small,
　　And why he didn't grow.

He slightly frowned, and with his eye
　　He looked me through and through—
"I'm just as big for me," said he,
　　"As you are big for you!"

John Kendrick Bangs

WARTIE THE FRIENDLY TROLL

Once upon a time, in a dark cave deep in the forest, there lived an ugly troll named Wartie. All trolls are ugly and the forest people went out of their way to avoid them, for not only were they ugly, they were also mean and nasty.

But Wartie was different. He wasn't mean or nasty. He was just ugly to look at. He wanted to be friendly, especially with the brownies who were his closest neighbors. But they were always so frightened of him that they ran away when they saw him. It made him very sad.

One day, Wartie looked at himself in the mirror for a long time.

"Well, no wonder the brownies are scared of me," he said to himself. "Why, I even scare myself a little! I'm as ugly as a troll can be, and there's nothing I can do to make myself even a teeny bit prettier."

And he sat down to ponder how and what he could do to make the brownies stop being afraid of him and maybe even like him.

Now, the brownies left their homes early every morning to go to work in the homes and farms nearby. They helped to churn the butter, weed the garden, wash the dishes, sweep and dust, run errands, and do hundreds of other chores. And, of course, they returned home very tired every evening.

One night, the brownies came home to find a jug of hot chocolate and a plate of cookies by their door. There was a note that read,

"Please leave the empties by the door." And it was signed, "A friend."

The hungry brownies were delighted. They drank the chocolate, ate the cookies, and pronounced it all delicious! And they wondered who the "friend" could be.

From that time on, every night when they came home they found a jug of hot chocolate and a plate of cookies waiting to welcome them. But they had no inkling as to who they could thank for such a kind and thoughtful deed.

Since no one had ever caught so much as a glimpse of the "friend," the brownies decided to take turns coming home early and hiding behind a bush near the door to watch.

Then, one moonlit night, the brownie
on watch stared in amazement as Wartie
lumbered slowly out of his dark cave.
He had a jug of hot chocolate
in one hand and a plate of cookies
in the other, and he put them down
gently by their door.

The brownie could hardly wait for
the others to return that night.

"I know who it is!" he shouted
as soon as he saw them. "And you'll
never, never guess! It's Wartie.
He's the one...What do you think
of that?"

The brownies could scarcely
believe their ears. They talked
excitedly as they ate the delicious
goodies.

"Who would ever believe a *troll* would do such a nice thing?"

"They're supposed to be mean and nasty! Why, Wartie isn't mean and nasty at all!"

"No, he's just ugly. And he can't help that!"

"To think we were afraid of him!"

"Let's go and thank him!"

With that, all the brownies trooped over to the dark cave and thanked Wartie for his kindness and thoughtfulness until tears of happiness ran like rivers down Wartie's face.

So the ugly but sweet Wartie and the brownies became fast friends and good neighbors forever after.

MY FAIRY FRIENDS

In the wonderful valley that never ends,
I love to look for my fairy friends,
To see their queer little heads pop out,
Quick as a flash, when no one's about.
Like lizards they lurk in the tufts of the grass
That shake suspiciously as I pass;
In the valley where purple crocuses grow,
They delight their silver horns to blow;
But creepy it is at the twilight hour,
When ghosts and goblins resume their power;
Then the twisted trunk of a common tree
Has arms and legs and a face to see:
But I'm not afraid, not a bit, not I!
For my fairy friends come floating by,
And they nod and they smile in their lovely way
At a little lost mortal, gone astray,
And with their protection I feel so strong
As if the whole world did to me belong!

Margaret Arndt